EMMANUEL JOSEPH

Voices Beyond Borders: Tales of Cultural Confluence

Copyright © 2025 by Emmanuel Joseph

All rights reserved. No part of this publication may be reproduced, stored or transmitted in any form or by any means, electronic, mechanical, photocopying, recording, scanning, or otherwise without written permission from the publisher. It is illegal to copy this book, post it to a website, or distribute it by any other means without permission.

First edition

*This book was professionally typeset on Reedsy.
Find out more at reedsy.com*

Contents

1	Chapter 1: The First Encounter	1
2	Chapter 2: A Symphony of Cultures	3
3	Chapter 3: The Culinary Diplomats	5
4	Chapter 4: The Cultural Ambassadors	7
5	Chapter 5: The Language of Peace	9
6	Chapter 6: The Global Entrepreneurs	11
7	Chapter 7: The Healing Hands	13
8	Chapter 8: The Cultural Custodians (continued)	15
9	Chapter 9: The Global Classroom	17
10	Chapter 10: The Diplomats of the Future	19
11	Chapter 11: The Power of Storytelling	21
12	Chapter 12: A Legacy of Unity	23
13	Chapter 13: The Cultural Revivalists	24
14	Chapter 14: The CrossCultural Innovators	26
15	Chapter 15: The Global Sports Ambassadors	28
16	Chapter 16: The Cultural Peacemakers	30
17	Chapter 17: The Cultural Researchers	32
18	Chapter 18: The Cultural Entrepreneurs	34
19	Chapter 19: The Cultural Environmentalists	36
20	Chapter 20: The Cultural Visionaries	38
21	Chapter 21: The Cultural Pioneers	40
22	Chapter 22: The CrossCultural Innovators	42
23	Chapter 23: The Cultural Educators	44
24	Chapter 24: The Global Storytellers	46

1

Chapter 1: The First Encounter

In a bustling market in Marrakech, the scent of exotic spices filled the air as tourists haggled with local vendors. Among them was Alex, a diplomat from Canada, who had come to experience the richness of Moroccan culture. His guide, Amina, spoke passionately about her homeland's history and traditions, bridging the gap between their vastly different worlds.

A few days later, Alex found himself invited to Amina's family home for a traditional Moroccan dinner. The warmth and hospitality he encountered there were beyond anything he had ever experienced. As they shared stories and laughter over couscous and tagine, Alex realized that this meal was not just about food—it was a symbol of trust and friendship.

Back in Canada, Alex began to incorporate elements of Moroccan culture into his diplomatic work. He introduced Moroccanthemed events and encouraged his colleagues to embrace crosscultural experiences. The impact was profound, fostering a deeper understanding and respect for different cultures within his team.

Years later, Amina visited Canada and was welcomed into Alex's home, just as he had been welcomed into hers. The bond they had formed transcended borders and became a testament to the power of cultural exchange.

Their friendship exemplified how personal connections can pave the way for international collaboration, breaking down barriers and building bridges. This story of an unexpected friendship became a model for others, showing that diplomacy starts with understanding and respect at a personal level.

2

Chapter 2: A Symphony of Cultures

At a music festival in Berlin, artists from around the world gathered to share their unique sounds. Among them was Hiroshi, a traditional Japanese shamisen player, and Maria, a flamenco guitarist from Spain. They had never met before, but their shared passion for music created an instant connection.

Their collaboration began as an experiment—melding the delicate, soulful notes of the shamisen with the fiery rhythms of the flamenco guitar. What emerged was a captivating fusion that resonated with audiences and transcended cultural boundaries.

The success of their performance led to an invitation to perform at various international venues. Each concert became a celebration of diversity, as they combined elements of their distinct musical traditions into a harmonious symphony.

In their travels, Hiroshi and Maria learned about each other's cultures and formed a deep mutual respect. They discovered that their music, though different in origin, shared common themes of love, struggle, and hope.

Their collaboration went beyond music; it inspired dialogues about cultural preservation and innovation. They encouraged young musicians to explore their cultural roots while embracing new influences, creating a global community united by the universal language of music.

Their story highlighted how cultural interactions could lead to creative breakthroughs and foster a sense of global unity. It reminded everyone that while our traditions may differ, our shared humanity is the melody that binds us together.

3

Chapter 3: The Culinary Diplomats

In the heart of New York City, a unique restaurant was born—a place where chefs from conflictridden regions came together to cook and share their cuisines. The brainchild of Anya, a peace advocate, and Tariq, a renowned chef, the restaurant aimed to promote peace through the universal language of food.

Each night, the restaurant's menu featured dishes from different cultures, prepared by chefs who once stood on opposite sides of political divides. Diners experienced the richness of these diverse culinary traditions, while the chefs shared their stories of resilience and hope.

One evening, an Israeli chef and a Palestinian chef found themselves working side by side. Initially, their interactions were marked by tension and suspicion. However, as they collaborated on a dish, they began to find common ground. They realized that their love for food and their desire for peace were stronger than their political differences.

Their partnership grew, and they started a cooking class that brought together people from different backgrounds. The kitchen became a place of dialogue and understanding, where food broke down barriers and built connections.

The restaurant's success inspired similar initiatives around the world. It showed that even in the face of conflict, cultural exchange could create spaces for reconciliation and unity. Through food, the chefs demonstrated that peace could be nurtured one meal at a time.

Their story served as a powerful reminder that cultural interactions could heal divides and build bridges, fostering a world where diversity is celebrated and unity is cherished.

4

Chapter 4: The Cultural Ambassadors

In a small village in Kenya, a group of young artists embarked on a mission to preserve their cultural heritage through art. They created stunning murals that depicted their history, traditions, and daily life, hoping to inspire pride and unity within their community.

Their work caught the attention of a global art organization, which invited them to participate in an international art exchange program. The artists traveled to various countries, sharing their culture and learning from others.

In India, they collaborated with local artists to create a mural that celebrated the connection between their two cultures. The artwork depicted scenes from both Kenyan and Indian life, showcasing the similarities and the beauty of their shared humanity.

As they traveled, the Kenyan artists realized the importance of cultural exchange in promoting mutual understanding and respect. They returned home with new perspectives and ideas, eager to continue their mission of cultural preservation and exchange.

Their journey inspired young people in their village to explore their cultural roots and express themselves through art. The murals they created became a source of pride and a symbol of the power of cultural confluence.

This story highlighted the role of artists as cultural ambassadors, bridging gaps and fostering connections through their work. It showed that through art, we could celebrate our diversity and unite as a global community.

5

Chapter 5: The Language of Peace

In a remote corner of the Himalayas, a small school was founded by Lhamo, a former monk, and Anita, a linguist from New Zealand. The school's mission was to teach children from different ethnic backgrounds, promoting peace and understanding through education.

The curriculum included lessons in multiple languages, reflecting the diverse cultures of the students. Lhamo and Anita believed that by learning each other's languages, the children would develop empathy and respect for different cultures.

One of the students, Tashi, came from a nomadic Tibetan family, while his best friend, Kiran, was from a farming community in Nepal. Initially, their cultural differences created misunderstandings, but the school's inclusive environment encouraged them to learn about each other's backgrounds.

Through language classes, Tashi and Kiran discovered the richness of their respective cultures and developed a deep friendship. They worked together on projects that celebrated their diversity, from traditional dance performances to storytelling sessions.

The school's impact extended beyond the students. Parents and community members began to see the value of cultural exchange and worked together to support the school's initiatives. The village became a model of peace and cooperation, demonstrating the power of education in fostering unity.

This story showcased how crosscultural interactions could be nurtured from a young age, creating a foundation for peaceful coexistence. It reminded us that by learning about each other's languages and cultures, we could build a more inclusive and harmonious world.

6

Chapter 6: The Global Entrepreneurs

In the bustling city of Lagos, Nigeria, a group of young entrepreneurs came together to create a tech startup that aimed to solve local problems with global solutions. The team was diverse, with members from different cultural backgrounds, each bringing unique perspectives and skills.

Their first project was a mobile app that connected local farmers with international markets, enabling them to sell their produce at fair prices. The app's success transformed the lives of many farmers, who could now support their families and communities.

As the startup grew, the team members learned from each other's cultures and developed a strong bond. They celebrated their differences and used them as a source of strength, finding innovative solutions to challenges they faced.

One of their most significant achievements was a partnership with a tech company in India, which helped them expand their reach and impact. The collaboration was a testament to the power of crosscultural interactions in driving innovation and progress.

The startup's success inspired other young entrepreneurs to embrace diversity and seek global partnerships. It showed that by working together and valuing each other's contributions, they could achieve remarkable things.

This story highlighted how cultural confluence could fuel entrepreneurship and create positive change. It reminded us that in today's interconnected world, our differences could be our greatest assets.

7

Chapter 7: The Healing Hands

In a refugee camp on the border of Jordan and Syria, a team of international doctors and nurses worked tirelessly to provide medical care to those in need. Among them were Dr. Ahmed, a Syrian surgeon, and Dr. Emily, a pediatrician from the United Kingdom.

Despite the language barriers and the challenging conditions, the medical team formed a closeknit community. They shared their knowledge and skills, learning from each other's medical practices and cultural traditions.

One day, a young girl named Aisha arrived at the camp with a severe injury. Dr. Ahmed and Dr. Emily worked together to treat her, combining their expertise to save her life. As Aisha recovered, they learned about her harrowing journey and her dreams for the future.

Their work went beyond medical care; they provided emotional support and a sense of hope to the refugees. The doctors and nurses became a source of comfort and strength, showing that compassion and empathy transcended cultural boundaries.

The medical team's dedication and unity inspired others to volunteer and support their mission. It showed that even in the most challenging circumstances, cultural interactions could bring healing and hope.

This story illustrated the power of crosscultural collaboration in times of crisis. It reminded us that by working together and caring for one another, we could make a difference in the world.

8

Chapter 8: The Cultural Custodians (continued)

Other's histories and traditions, finding commonalities that transcended their differences. They discovered that their shared passion for history and preservation could bridge gaps and foster unity.

Their work faced challenges, from political tensions to funding issues, but their commitment to preserving Jerusalem's heritage never wavered. They organized educational programs and community events, inviting people from different backgrounds to learn about and appreciate the city's rich cultural tapestry.

One of their most significant achievements was the restoration of a historic synagogue that had been damaged during a conflict. The project brought together Jewish, Christian, and Muslim volunteers, who worked side by side to restore the building. Their collaboration became a symbol of hope and reconciliation, demonstrating that cultural preservation could promote peace and unity.

Their story highlighted the importance of preserving cultural heritage as a means of fostering understanding and respect among different communities. It reminded us that by working together to protect our shared history, we could build a more inclusive and harmonious world.

9

Chapter 9: The Global Classroom

In a small village in Peru, a group of teachers launched an innovative educational program that connected students from around the world through virtual classrooms. The program aimed to promote cultural exchange and global understanding by allowing students to learn about each other's countries and traditions.

The students, from diverse backgrounds, participated in online discussions, shared projects, and collaborated on assignments. Through these interactions, they developed a deeper appreciation for different cultures and formed lasting friendships.

One of the most impactful projects was a cultural exchange day, where students from different countries shared their traditional music, dances, and stories. The event celebrated diversity and showcased the beauty of cultural confluence.

The program's success inspired other schools to adopt similar initiatives, creating a global network of interconnected classrooms. The students' experiences in the virtual classroom fostered a sense of global citizenship, encouraging them to become ambassadors of peace and understanding.

This story demonstrated the power of education in promoting crosscultural interactions and building a more inclusive world. It reminded us that by connecting with each other and sharing our stories, we could create a global community united by mutual respect and understanding.

10

Chapter 10: The Diplomats of the Future

In the halls of the United Nations, a new generation of diplomats was emerging—young leaders who understood the importance of cultural confluence in international relations. Among them were Zara from Nigeria and Rafael from Brazil, who had met during their studies at a prestigious international relations program.

Their diverse backgrounds and experiences shaped their approach to diplomacy, emphasizing the need for cultural sensitivity and inclusivity. They believed that by understanding and respecting different cultures, they could build stronger, more effective international partnerships.

Zara and Rafael worked together on various initiatives, from climate change negotiations to peacebuilding efforts. Their collaborative approach and cultural awareness earned them the respect of their peers and superiors.

One of their most significant achievements was the establishment of a cultural exchange program that brought together young leaders from different countries to share their experiences and learn from each other. The program became a model for fostering crosscultural understanding and collaboration.

Their story highlighted the importance of cultural confluence in shaping the future of international relations. It showed that by embracing diversity and promoting inclusivity, we could build a more peaceful and prosperous world.

11

Chapter 11: The Power of Storytelling

In a small town in Ireland, a group of writers came together to create an anthology of stories that celebrated cultural confluence. The project, led by Aisling, a renowned author, aimed to showcase how crosscultural interactions shaped and defined their community.

The writers, from diverse backgrounds, shared their personal stories of cultural exchange, highlighting the beauty and challenges of living in a multicultural society. The anthology featured tales of love, friendship, and resilience, demonstrating the transformative power of cultural interactions.

One of the most poignant stories was about a young immigrant who found a sense of belonging through a local storytelling group. Through the power of words, he connected with his new community and shared his experiences, fostering empathy and understanding.

The anthology's success inspired other communities to create their own collections of stories, celebrating the richness of their cultural diversity. It showed that storytelling could be a powerful tool for promoting crosscultural understanding and unity.

This story underscored the importance of sharing our stories and experiences as a means of fostering connection and empathy. It reminded us that through storytelling, we could bridge gaps and build a more inclusive world.

12

Chapter 12: A Legacy of Unity

As the years passed, the stories of cultural confluence continued to shape and define international relations. The individuals and communities who embraced crosscultural interactions left a lasting legacy of unity and understanding.

From the diplomats who fostered international collaboration to the artists who celebrated cultural diversity, their efforts created a more inclusive and harmonious world. Their stories served as a reminder that our shared humanity transcended borders and that through cultural exchange, we could build a better future.

As new generations emerged, they were inspired by the stories of those who had come before them. They carried forward the torch of cultural confluence, continuing to promote mutual respect and understanding in their communities and beyond.

This anthology of stories highlighted the profound impact of crosscultural interactions on international relations. It showed that by embracing diversity and celebrating our shared humanity, we could create a world where unity and peace flourished.

13

Chapter 13: The Cultural Revivalists

In a quaint village in the Italian countryside, a group of elders embarked on a mission to revive their cultural heritage. They organized festivals, workshops, and performances that celebrated their traditions, hoping to pass them on to the younger generation.

The initiative, led by Antonio, a retired teacher, and Sophia, a young artist, brought together people of all ages. They shared stories, songs, and dances that had been passed down through generations, ensuring that their cultural legacy would endure.

One of their most significant achievements was the creation of a cultural center that served as a hub for community activities. The center hosted events that showcased the village's rich history and traditions, attracting visitors from near and far.

Through their efforts, the villagers developed a renewed sense of pride in their heritage. They realized that their traditions were not just relics of the past, but living expressions of their identity and resilience.

This story highlighted the importance of preserving cultural heritage and the role of community in keeping traditions alive. It reminded us that by celebrating our cultural roots, we could strengthen our connections and build a more cohesive society.

14

Chapter 14: The CrossCultural Innovators

In the bustling tech hub of Seoul, South Korea, a group of engineers and designers from different countries collaborated on a groundbreaking project. Their goal was to create a smart device that could seamlessly integrate into various cultural contexts, enhancing the user experience for people around the world.

The team, led by Jinsoo, a visionary engineer, and Maria, a creative designer, approached the project with a deep appreciation for cultural diversity. They conducted extensive research, learning about the preferences and needs of users from different backgrounds.

Their collaboration resulted in a device that was not only technologically advanced but also culturally sensitive. It featured customizable interfaces and multilingual support, making it accessible and userfriendly for people from diverse cultures.

The device's success demonstrated the power of crosscultural collaboration in driving innovation. It showed that by valuing and incorporating diverse perspectives, we could create products that truly served a global audience.

CHAPTER 14: THE CROSSCULTURAL INNOVATORS

This story highlighted the role of cultural confluence in shaping the future of technology. It reminded us that in our interconnected world, innovation thrives when we embrace and celebrate our differences.

15

Chapter 15: The Global Sports Ambassadors

On the soccer fields of Rio de Janeiro, a group of young athletes from different countries gathered for an international sports camp. The camp, organized by a nonprofit organization, aimed to promote crosscultural understanding and unity through the universal language of sports.

The athletes, from diverse backgrounds, shared a common passion for soccer. They trained together, learning new techniques and strategies from each other. Through friendly matches and teambuilding activities, they developed a sense of camaraderie and mutual respect.

One of the highlights of the camp was a cultural exchange day, where the athletes showcased their traditional dances, music, and cuisine. The event celebrated their diversity and demonstrated the power of sports in fostering cultural connections.

The friendships formed at the camp extended beyond the soccer field. The athletes stayed in touch, supporting each other's endeavors and promoting cultural understanding in their communities.

CHAPTER 15: THE GLOBAL SPORTS AMBASSADORS

This story showcased the role of sports in bringing people together and promoting global unity. It reminded us that through shared experiences and mutual respect, we could build a world where diversity is celebrated and differences are embraced.

16

Chapter 16: The Cultural Peacemakers

In the conflictridden region of the Middle East, a group of peace activists from different cultural backgrounds came together to promote dialogue and reconciliation. Their mission was to foster understanding and cooperation among communities divided by years of conflict.

The group, led by Leila, a humanitarian worker, and David, a conflict resolution expert, organized workshops and peacebuilding initiatives that encouraged people to share their stories and perspectives. They believed that by listening to each other and acknowledging their shared humanity, they could pave the way for lasting peace.

One of their most impactful initiatives was a storytelling project that brought together individuals from different sides of the conflict. Through their stories, participants discovered common experiences and aspirations, breaking down barriers and building connections.

The group's efforts inspired others to join the movement for peace and reconciliation. It showed that even in the most challenging circumstances, cultural interactions could create spaces for dialogue and understanding.

This story highlighted the importance of crosscultural interactions in conflict resolution and peacebuilding. It reminded us that by promoting empathy and mutual respect, we could create a more peaceful and harmonious world.

17

Chapter 17: The Cultural Researchers

In a university in Singapore, a team of researchers embarked on a groundbreaking study to explore the impact of cultural interactions on global health. Led by Dr. Chen, an epidemiologist, and Dr. Patel, a sociologist, the study aimed to understand how cultural practices influenced health outcomes and behaviors.

The researchers conducted fieldwork in different countries, learning about traditional healing practices, dietary habits, and health beliefs. They discovered that cultural interactions played a significant role in shaping health behaviors and outcomes.

One of their most significant findings was the positive impact of cultural exchange on mental health. They observed that individuals who engaged in crosscultural interactions reported higher levels of wellbeing and resilience.

The study's results were published in a prestigious journal, sparking a global conversation about the importance of cultural sensitivity in healthcare. It inspired healthcare professionals to adopt a more holistic and inclusive approach to patient care.

This story showcased the role of cultural interactions in advancing our understanding of global health. It reminded us that by valuing and respecting different cultural perspectives, we could improve health outcomes and promote wellbeing for all.

18

Chapter 18: The Cultural Entrepreneurs

In the vibrant city of Mumbai, India, a group of social entrepreneurs launched a project that aimed to empower women from marginalized communities through cultural exchange and economic opportunities. The project, called "EmpowerHer," provided training and support for women to start their own businesses.

The entrepreneurs, led by Priya, a passionate advocate for women's rights, and Ayesha, a successful businesswoman, believed that cultural exchange could be a powerful tool for empowerment. They organized workshops that combined traditional crafts with modern business skills, enabling women to create and market their products.

One of their most successful initiatives was a cultural fair that showcased the women's handmade crafts and products. The event attracted visitors from different countries, fostering crosscultural interactions and promoting the women's businesses.

Through their efforts, the women gained confidence and financial independence, transforming their lives and communities. The project's success inspired similar initiatives in other regions, demonstrating the impact of cultural exchange on economic empowerment.

CHAPTER 18: THE CULTURAL ENTREPRENEURS

This story highlighted the importance of cultural confluence in promoting social and economic development. It reminded us that by empowering marginalized communities and celebrating their cultural contributions, we could create a more inclusive and equitable world.

19

Chapter 19: The Cultural Environmentalists

In the lush rainforests of the Amazon, a group of environmentalists from different countries collaborated on a project to protect the region's biodiversity. The project, led by Dr. Carlos, a Brazilian ecologist, and Dr. Mei, a Chinese conservationist, aimed to promote sustainable practices and raise awareness about the importance of preserving the rainforest.

The team conducted research on the region's unique flora and fauna, learning from the indigenous communities about their traditional knowledge and conservation practices. They discovered that cultural interactions played a crucial role in promoting environmental sustainability.

One of their most impactful initiatives was a communitybased conservation program that involved local villagers in protecting the rainforest. The project combined scientific research with traditional practices, creating a model for sustainable development.

The team's efforts garnered international recognition, highlighting the importance of cultural confluence in environmental conservation. It showed that by working together and respecting indigenous knowledge, we could

CHAPTER 19: THE CULTURAL ENVIRONMENTALISTS

protect our planet's natural heritage.

This story showcased the role of cultural interactions in promoting environmental sustainability. It reminded us that by valuing and incorporating diverse perspectives, we could create a more sustainable and harmonious world.

20

Chapter 20: The Cultural Visionaries

In a futuristic city, a group of visionaries from different cultural backgrounds came together to imagine and create a world where cultural confluence was celebrated and embraced. Their vision was to build a society where diversity was seen as a strength and crosscultural interactions were the norm.

The visionaries, led by Maya, a renowned architect, and Rafael, a tech innovator, designed a city that reflected their values. The city's architecture, technology, and public spaces were all infused with elements from different cultures, creating a vibrant and inclusive environment.

One of their most significant achievements was the creation of a cultural hub that served as a center for learning, collaboration, and celebration. The hub hosted events that showcased the city's diversity, from cultural festivals to art exhibitions.

The city became a model for others, demonstrating the power of cultural confluence in shaping a more inclusive and harmonious society. It showed that by embracing our differences and celebrating our shared humanity, we could create a brighter future for all.

CHAPTER 20: THE CULTURAL VISIONARIES

This story highlighted the importance of visionary thinking in promoting cultural confluence. It reminded us that by imagining and building a world where diversity is celebrated, we could create a more inclusive and peaceful society.

And that concludes the anthology of stories in "Voices Beyond Borders: Tales of Cultural Confluence." I hope these tales inspire you and highlight the transformative power of crosscultural interactions in shaping our world. If there's anything else you'd like to discuss or explore, feel free to let me know.

21

Chapter 21: The Cultural Pioneers

In the thriving metropolis of Tokyo, a group of entrepreneurs from different cultural backgrounds embarked on a mission to create a crosscultural coworking space. The space, named "Global Hub," aimed to foster collaboration, innovation, and mutual understanding among professionals from around the world.

The founders, led by Yuki, a tech entrepreneur, and Isabella, a marketing strategist, designed the space to reflect their values of inclusivity and diversity. They incorporated elements from different cultures into the design, creating a vibrant and welcoming environment.

One of the most successful initiatives at Global Hub was the "Cultural Exchange Nights," where members shared their traditions, cuisines, and experiences. These events became a highlight of the community, fostering friendships and professional collaborations.

The coworking space thrived, attracting professionals from various industries and backgrounds. The diverse community became a source of inspiration and innovation, demonstrating the power of crosscultural collaboration.

This story highlighted the importance of creating inclusive spaces that

CHAPTER 21: THE CULTURAL PIONEERS

celebrate diversity. It reminded us that by embracing our differences, we could foster creativity and drive positive change in our communities.

22

Chapter 22: The CrossCultural Innovators

In the bustling city of Nairobi, Kenya, a group of young innovators from different countries came together to tackle pressing social issues through technology. Their startup, "TechForGood," focused on developing solutions that addressed challenges such as access to education, healthcare, and clean water.

The team, led by David, a software engineer, and Amara, a social entrepreneur, approached each project with a deep appreciation for cultural diversity. They conducted fieldwork in different communities, learning about the local context and involving community members in the design process.

One of their most impactful projects was a mobile app that connected rural communities with essential services. The app's success demonstrated the potential of technology to bridge gaps and improve lives.

The startup's collaborative approach and cultural sensitivity earned them recognition and support from global organizations. Their work became a model for using technology to create positive social impact.

CHAPTER 22: THE CROSSCULTURAL INNOVATORS

This story showcased the role of cultural confluence in driving innovation and addressing global challenges. It reminded us that by working together and valuing diverse perspectives, we could create solutions that truly make a difference.

23

Chapter 23: The Cultural Educators

In a university in Amsterdam, a group of professors from different disciplines launched a groundbreaking course on cultural confluence. The course, called "Global Perspectives," aimed to explore the impact of crosscultural interactions on various aspects of society.

The professors, led by Dr. Ibrahim, an anthropologist, and Dr. Li, a historian, designed the course to be interdisciplinary and inclusive. They invited guest speakers from different cultural backgrounds to share their experiences and insights.

The students, from diverse countries, engaged in lively discussions and collaborative projects. They explored topics such as migration, global trade, and cultural heritage, gaining a deeper understanding of the interconnectedness of the world.

One of the most memorable projects was a research trip to a multicultural neighborhood in Amsterdam, where students conducted interviews and documented their findings. The experience highlighted the richness and complexity of cultural interactions in a global city.

The course's success inspired other universities to adopt similar programs, promoting crosscultural understanding and collaboration in higher education.

This story highlighted the importance of education in fostering cultural confluence. It reminded us that by learning about and appreciating different cultures, we could build a more inclusive and interconnected world.

24

Chapter 24: The Global Storytellers

In the heart of London, a group of filmmakers and writers from different countries came together to create a documentary series that celebrated cultural confluence. The series, called "Global Voices," aimed to showcase the stories of individuals who had experienced the transformative power of crosscultural interactions.

The team, led by Emma, a filmmaker, and Raj, a journalist, traveled to various countries, capturing the diverse and inspiring stories of people who had built bridges across cultural divides. They documented tales of friendship, collaboration, and resilience, highlighting the beauty and strength of cultural diversity.

One of the most powerful episodes featured the story of a refugee artist who found a new home and community through his art. His journey of overcoming adversity and building connections through creativity resonated with audiences worldwide.

The documentary series received critical acclaim and sparked conversations about the importance of cultural confluence in today's world. It showed that through storytelling, we could celebrate our shared humanity and inspire others to embrace diversity.

CHAPTER 24: THE GLOBAL STORYTELLERS

This story underscored the role of media and storytelling in promoting crosscultural understanding. It reminded us that by sharing our stories and listening to others, we could build a more inclusive and compassionate world.

And with that, the anthology "Voices Beyond Borders: Tales of Cultural Confluence" comes to an end. These stories have highlighted the transformative power of crosscultural interactions in shaping our world. I hope they inspire you to celebrate diversity and embrace the beauty of our shared humanity. If there's anything else you'd like to explore or discuss, I'm here for you.

www.ingramcontent.com/pod-product-compliance
Lightning Source LLC
LaVergne TN
LVHW012129070526
838202LV00056B/5933